Deadly Durham

A grisly guided walk around the old city with
terribly true (*well, mainly true*) tales

Terry Deary

Illustrations by David Boyes

COUNTY DURHAM BOOKS

The author would like to especially thank Carolyn Ball, the staff of the County Record Office, and Debbie Rowley-Conwy for their invaluable assistance in researching material for this book.

Photographs/Engravings pages 4, 5, 12, 19, 20, 29 © County Record Office, Durham
(NB The reference letters/numbers alongside these images will identify them at the County Record Office)

Additional photographs © Peter Rowley-Conwy

Published by County Durham Books, 2001
ISBN 1 897585 64 0

INTRODUCTION

There's History ... and there's *history*.

There's History - that deadly dry, brain-dulling collection of dates and data that teachers taught and tested you on at school.

Then there's the really important stuff. The old stories. The terrific tales of real people who lived in olden days. Tales of heroes and daring deeds - tales of villains and dreadful deeds. That's what real history is about. People.

You're probably a person. So you want to read about people just like you. Ordinary people who did extraordinary things.

Never mind the maths and science and English they try to teach you at school. They don't matter much. There is just one subject you need to learn. People.

And there is just one exam question you need to answer when you leave school. "Why do people behave the way they do?"

HI! I'M TERRY. WHAT'S YOUR NAME?

Once you can answer that question you are ready to answer the BIG question in life: "Why do *I* behave the way *I* do?"

And there's one subject that will help you to answer that question more than any other - *history*.

Of course it helps if you can visit the places where the terrific tales took place.

An old city like Durham has hundreds of superb stories. Read the stories at the places where they happened and they come to life - many of the people in the stories come to life, too. Many more come to *death*.

For, in its thousand years of history, Durham has had its share of dreadful deaths, too. Durham has been a pretty deadly place. Deadly Durham. Hey! That's a good title for a book. A book like this ...

3

How to use the book

There are fourteen sites chosen. They are linked by a walk that will take you about an hour (if you are in a hurry) or half a day if you want to wander a little. (There is also a map, on page 52, to help you.)

Stop at each one and read the stories linked to the place. And read some of the other fascinating facts about the age.

Those fourteen sites are arranged roughly in order of date - so you start at the beginning of Durham and end up around a hundred years ago.

Not only are you walking through a space called Durham - you are also walking through time.

Step aboard your time machine and go back to the earliest days of Durham.

CHAPTER 1

A COFFIN AND A COW

Durham Cathedral

On this spot ...Durham began.

On the wall of the Cathedral you can see the carving of a woman milking a cow. That was carved around 1775. It replaced a much older carving made around 1100.

The first church on this spot was built as a resting place for Saint Cuthbert's coffin. The city grew around the church. In 1074 a monastery grew around the church too. In 1093 the church was replaced by the Cathedral - complete with carved cow. But why a carved cow?

The cow carving is explained by the old legend ...

The story of lost monks and a lost cow

dph324-61

The old story says Saint Cuthbert lived, died and was buried at Lindisfarne Island off the Northumberland coast. But around the year 875 vicious Vikings raided the monastery there and the monks fled - taking Cuthbert's coffin with them.

The monks carried the coffin around the north for seven years and then settled in Chester-le-Street for 113 years. The vicious Vikings attacked again in 995, the monks fled with St Cuthbert's body and finally reached a hill called Ward-lawe. They were exhausted and dejected and found they couldn't move the coffin. It seemed to be glued to the ground. A miracle and a message - but what

5

message? The bewildered monks fasted and prayed for three days till they had a vision that said, "Bury Cuthbert at Dunholme."

But the monks were strangers. They had no idea where Dunholme was. Quite by chance they heard a milk-maid call to her friend, "I've lost my cow. You haven't seen her, have you?"

And the friend said, "Yes. I saw her over at Dunholme." A second miracle.

The monks asked her exactly where Dunholme was and the woman led them to it. The spot was covered in forest at that time. The monks built a small wooden church and buried the old saint inside.

Nearly a hundred years later the Normans took down the wooden church and started to build the cathedral you see there today. All because of a wandering cow.

Nice story, but ... what was a cow doing looking for food in a forest? The forest was described as a "barbarous and rough place full of nothing but thorn bushes and thick wood". How did the cow get through the bushes? Cows prefer grass.

The cow story was probably a local legend made up after the cathedral was built.

Five foul facts about vicious Vikings

1. In 793 AD there were reports of fiery dragons in the skies of the north. A sign of disaster. Sure enough, the Vikings first arrived in the north that year when they attacked Lindisfarne monastery - a pretty soft target for such hard men. They robbed the monks and took some slaves - then they went home for the winter.

2. In 851 they came to settle. By 865 they were asking for "Danegeld" - protection money. "Pay us Danegeld or we will burn your homes and batter you to death." The English paid up ... so the Danes come back for more. In 871 King Alfred the Great (or Alfred the Cake, if you prefer) drove the Danes from the South-West of England - but in the North-East the people are stuck with Viking rulers for another couple of hundred years. Thanks for nothing Alf.

3. The Vikings enjoyed nothing better than a long "epic" poem to listen to as they sat around their fires on a winter night. But these poems could be pretty vicious. Like the one about a Viking warrior who boasts:

I have held a sword and spear when they were slippery with blood.
Hawks were hovering at the hill as bravely the violent Vikings stood.
Red flames swallowed up men's roofs as we cut them down;
Bodies, skewered, lay there sleepy in the gateways to the town

4. The Vikings didn't always win. After the Lindisfarne raid they decided to attack Jarrow monastery on the Tyne. Bad weather held up their landing so the Jarrow folk were ready for the invaders when they landed. The Viking leader was captured and sent back to his ship - he was in a box and chopped up into lots of pieces. The Vikings stayed away for the next forty years - they sailed all the way to Ireland for easier targets.

5. It wasn't a lot of fun being a horse in Viking times. Some were fitted with sharpened shoes and trained to fight other horses for sport. And, of course, Vikings quite enjoyed eating horse meat. They also ate seagulls, polar bears and whales.

CHAPTER 2

SAINTS AND SMITHS

St Cuthbert's tomb

On this spot ... St Cuthbert is buried.

Saint Cuthbert died at around the age of fifty-five and his coffin was taken around the north till a suitable burial place was found. The coffin went as far south as Fishlake, South Yorkshire and as far north as Melrose in the Scottish borders.

The first coffin was made of wood and the monks carried it as lightly as a spider's web on wagons and on boats across rivers.

But Saint Cuthbert was not allowed to rest in peace, as the old story tells us ...

The story of the uncorrupted corpse

Saint Cuthbert may have been dead, but he wasn't some dusty skeleton. A book of 1593 tells the tale:

"In 1538 the sacred shrine of holy Saint Cuthbert was vandalised during a visit by a Doctor Ley, a Doctor Henley, and a Mr. Blythma. They were in Durham to carry out the destruction of such monuments for King Henry VIII. It was their job to take away any riches of gold jewels. After they'd taken of Cuthbert's ornaments and jewels, they came nearer to his coffin, expecting to find nothing but dust and bones. Finding Cuthbert's coffin very strongly bound with iron then they took a great blacksmith's hammer and broke into the chest. And when they had opened the lid they found Cuthbert lying whole, uncorrupted with his face bare. His beard was as if it had been a fortnight growth, and all his robes he wore in church: and his stick of gold lying beside him. Then when one of the breakers noticed that he had broken one of Cuthbert's legs when he did break open the coffin; the man was very sorry for it and did cry, 'Alas I have broke one of his legs.'"

The story went around that Saint Cuthbert's body had not rotted – it was a saintly miracle.

The truth is that Cuthbert's body may have been mummified after he died. Henry VIII's body-snatchers could well have seen a body and not a skeleton.

Five fantastic facts about St Cuthbert

1. The monk, Simeon of Durham, wrote: "William the Conqueror came into Durham, and asked if the body of Cuthbert rested there. Everyone swore that was true yet William would not believe them.

"The king decided that if Cuthbert's holy body were not discovered there, he would order all the chief nobles and monks to be beheaded.

"The king was just about to carry out his threat when suddenly he was overcome with an awful heat, so powerful that he could hardly bear it. He rushed to leave the church, hurriedly mounted his horse, and did not stop until he had reached the river Tees."

2. Saint Oswald died forty-five years before Cuthbert at the Battle of Maserfield in 642 AD. Oswald's body was chopped to pieces by Penda, the King of Mercia and his head was stuck up on a pole. King Oswy later took the head down and carried it to Lindisfarne monastery. When the monks fled with the body of Cuthbert, they took Oswald's head as well. In 1104 the head was said to be by the side of St Cuthbert keeping him company in the coffin.

A skull has been found in the coffin and that could well be the head of Oswald. It has signs of a violent death, with a tremendous cut across the skull, from a sharp axe or sword, in keeping with death in battle.

3. The coffin was opened again in 1827. They found bones closely wrapped in ancient robes. They also found several valuable relics of St. Cuthbert (missed by Henry VIII's grave robbers.). They included the cross of St Cuthbert, a portable altar, an ivory comb and a ring. These valuable items were taken to the cathedral library.

4. A report of 1899 said "It was noticed by Canon Fowler that in one of the eye sockets of the skull was a something of which he says, 'I have no doubt that it was a shrivelled eyeball, including the lids. If this is so, it is surely strong confirmation that the body had been mummified.' When the bones were taken out for us it was found that only one important part was missing, one of the thigh bones." This may be the "leg" which was broken by the goldsmith with his hammer.

Dr. Selby Plummer says that "the age of the skeleton at death was about fifty-five years of age," - St. Cuthbert's age at his death. And finally, reports tell us that St. Cuthbert was "neither very tall nor very short, and the skeleton as we carefully measured it was about five feet eight inches long. These findings tell us that here we almost certainly have the remains of St. Cuthbert."

5. St Cuthbert performed so many healing miracles that he became known as the "wonderworker of Britain". People also believed he talked to birds (an eagle brought him food), to animals (otters wiped his feet dry with their fur) and to angels (who came to dinner with him); he drove out devils; put out a fire with a prayer; drew water from dry ground; cured the sick ... and saw into the future - including his own death.

CHAPTER 3

BEDE'S BONES

Bede's tomb

On this spot...the famous monk and historian, Bede, is buried.

People used to work out the year by the reign of the monarch ... so 2002, say, would be "the 50th year of Elizabeth II's reign". Bede said, "We should work time out from the date of the birth of Jesus." So he did. And we still do. Much easier.

Bede said the world was round when everyone else thought it was flat. No one has fallen off the edge yet, so he must have been right.

And Bede wrote the first history of the English people. The times he lived in are known as The Dark Ages because we know so little about what happened. Without Bede we'd have known even *less* about the English and where they came from.

Sadly he didn't write much about *himself*.

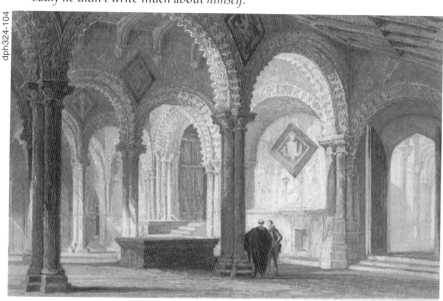

dph324-104

Today, his tomb can be seen in the Galilee Chapel of Durham Cathedral. But how did it get there?

The story of Bede's bones

Monks in the Middle Ages were very superstitious. They believed that all sorts of holy objects were magical. The bones of dead saints were treasured. So it's no surprise the bones of Bede were more valuable than a chest of gold – and that they were stolen.

Simeon of Durham tells the story ...

"In 1022 a monk called Alfred had a dream. In this dream he was ordered by God to visit the old monasteries in the north and dig up the bones of the saints who were buried there. They were to be shown to the people and worshipped.

It was Alfred's custom to visit the monastery of Jarrow (in which he knew Bede had lived, died, and was buried).

Alfred went as usual and, (after spending some days there within the church alone, praying, and watching) very early in the morning he returned alone to Durham. (This was a thing which he had never done before.)

No one saw him leave but the monks soon realised Bede's bones had gone. For years Alfred never returned to Jarrow. Friends often asked him where the Venerable Bede was resting and Alfred's usual answer was always the same: "No one knows better about this than I do. The same coffin which holds the most holy body of the father Cuthbert, contains also the bones of the teacher and monk Bede."

Having spoken, he begged his friends to keep the matter quiet in case the bones were stolen again.

Five foul facts about miserable monks

Bede was a Saxon monk living in the days before the Vikings attacked. But, even without Vikings it was a hard life.

1. Monks removed the hair from the top of their heads. But they didn't have razors. First they cut off the hair with a small pair of shears then they rubbed the rest off with a stone - called a pumice stone - until there was no hair left on top. Rub too hard and you rubbed the skin off. Even if you survived the haircut you'd have a very cold head in winter.

2. The monks were among the few people who could write in Saxon times. Bede himself wrote books about the Bible and books about the saints, apart from his famous history book. But writing wasn't always an easy job. The Abbot of Monkwearmouth wrote a letter to a friend in Germany and said :
"During the past winter our island has been savagely troubled with cold and ice and with long and widespread storms of wind and rain. It is so bad that the hand of the writers become numb and cannot produce a very large number of books."

3. A good monk spent many hours praying, night and day, as well as working in the monastery garden to make food. Monks also acted as the area doctors. But some of the cures were curious. They said ...
For toothache - boil a holly leaf, lay it on a saucer of water, raise the saucer to your mouth and yawn. The worms causing the toothache will come tumbling out.
For madness - take the skin of a dolphin, make it into a whip, beat the mad person with the whip and they will soon be cured.
Bede was a boy at Jarrow monastery on the Tyne when the local people suffered from a plague. They came to the monastery for a cure - and spread the plague to the monks. Only Bede and his abbot survived. Dangerous doctoring.

4. Even miserable monks enjoyed a joke. One of the most popular Saxon pastimes

was creating "riddles" for friends to solve. A riddle written by a monk in Bede's time went like this . . .

Q: What has two ears and one eye, two feet and 1201 heads, one belly, one back, one pair of hands and arms and one neck?

A   A one-eyed garlic seller with 1200 heads of garlic to sell.

5. Not every monastery was filled with caring monks.

Bede told the story of Coldingham monastery in Northumbria. The monastery was destroyed by fire in 679 AD. A Celt called Adamnan warned that he had a dream in which he saw the monastery destroyed. "The monks cells that were built for praying have been turned into places of feasting and drinking." The Coldingham monks behaved themselves for a while after Adamnan's warning. Then they went back to their old ways and Bede said the fire was sent by God as their punishment.

CHAPTER 4

WICKED WOMEN

The Gallilee Chapel

On this spot ... women were allowed to worship in the Cathedral.

The problem was that women were seen as a bit wicked. They made the monks forget about their study and their prayers.

Coldingham monastery was for nuns as well as monks. When the monks turned to feasting, drinking, talking ... and other wickedness then God burned the monastery down. Of course the women got the blame. (Nothing changes.)

So, women were not welcome in the Cathedral. But the monks agreed they had to have somewhere to worship - a "Lady" chapel. (Not a chapel for ladies. But a chapel where they could worship The Lady Mary, Jesus' mother.)

The story of the Cuthbert's cursed chapel

The Lady Chapel is now at the west end of the cathedral. But it was *meant* to be at the east end. Bishop Pudsey even started building a Lady Chapel at the east end.

Who stopped him?

Saint Cuthbert ... who'd been dead hundreds of years.

How did woman-hating Cuthbert do this? A 1593 report explains:

"Bishop Hugh Pudsey decided that there should be a chapel where women could worship and he began to build one at the east end of the Cathedral church. Several marble pillars were put up but they soon began to crack and fall down. It was clear that Saint Cuthbert did not like the new chapel because it meant women would be allowed too near his coffin. So the work was abandoned and a new Lady Chapel was built at the west end of the church."

A true story? Partly. The first chapel *did* collapse. But don't blame Cuthbert. Why? Cracks were almost certainly due to faulty foundations. Most of the cathedral is built on solid rock. This falls away sharply at the east end where the lady Chapel was first erected.

So the collapsing chapel was down to bad builders, not a sabotaging saint or wicked women.

Five fantastic facts about foul female life

1. Cuthbert had never liked women. On Lindisfarne they didn't simply have a separate chapel - they had a separate *church* built for them - 'Grene Cyrice' (Green Church). Cuthbert's body had rested in several churches on its escape from Lindisfarne to Durham. A law was passed that said women weren't even allowed to set foot in the graveyards around those churches, never mind the church itself.

2. A Durham woman called Sungeova was returning home one evening from a night out with her husband. She never stopped complaining about the road." Its' full of potholes and puddles," she moaned. "I can't keep my skirts clean."

So at last she decided that they should take a short-cut through the churchyard of Durham Cathedral - even though women were banned.

As she entered she was gripped with some kind of invisible horror. She cried out, "I am losing my mind."

Her husband moaned, "Come on, woman. There's nothing to be afraid of."

But as soon as she staggered outside the hedge that surrounds the cemetery she fell down.

Friends helped her husband to carry her home ... but Sungeova was dead. Cruel Cuthbert's curse?

3. But a queen survived. In 1333 King Edward III arrived at Durham on his march north to fight the Scots. A few days after, Queen Philippa came from Knaresborough to meet him, and went through the abbey gates to the priory where he was staying. After dining with the king Philippa went to bed. The monks were frantic. One went to the king and told him that St. Cuthbert had a deadly hatred of women in the area round the cathedral. Edward immediately ordered the queen to get up. Philippa, in her underclothes hurried through the gate and went to stay in the castle. The queen prayed long and hard for Cuthbert to forgive her. She survived. Maybe Cuthbert was softer on queens.

brank

Two ancient punishments of Newcastle, inflicted on disturbers of the peace, appear as being practised about this time. A common drunkard was led through the streets as a spectacle of contempt, covered with a large barrel, called a "*Newcastle Cloak*," one end being out and the other having a hole made through it, sufficient for the offender to pass his head through, by which means the vessel rested on his shoulders. The scold wore an iron engine called "*the branks*," in the form of a crown, it covered the head,
VOL. 1.   P

4. Women had their own punishments in the Middle Ages. Ann Runcorn's crime was to nag her husband in public, calling him "villain" and "rogue". Ann was fitted with a cage over her head - an instrument called a "brank". A metal rod poked into her mouth to hold down her tongue. Ann was then placed upon a horse facing backwards, and led through the market where people could mock her and throw dirt at her. A brank was still being used in Shrewsbury in 1846.

5. Cuthbert wasn't alone as a holy hater of women. The Norman priest Robert d'Abrissel said, "A woman is a witch, a snake, a plague, a rat, a rash, a poison, a burning flame and an assistant of the Devil." Whew.

CHAPTER 5

FIRE AND FURY

Palace Green

On this spot ... the first Norman Earl to arrive in Durham was killed.

William the Conqueror gave the job of ruling Durham to the Earl of Northumberland, Robert Cumyn. He was a ruthless man and the Durham people feared for their lives.

It was kill or be killed.

The Durham people killed.

Perhaps they wouldn't have been so vicious if they'd known how ruthless William the Conqueror's revenge was going to be.

View of Durham Castle being the Bishops Palace

The story of the killing of Cumyn

Simeon of Durham reported:

"When the people of Durham heard Cumyn was on his way they planned to escape. But a fierce snowstorm and a harsh frost stopped them. They then decided instead to either murder the earl ... or die in the attempt.

"The bishop of Durham warned the earl and advised him to stay away. Cumyn ignored the advice and entered Durham with 700 men, determined to punish the rebels. The people suffered and any man who raised a weapon against a Norman was butchered.

"Then, very early in the morning of 31 January the rebels broke in through all the gates, and running through the city, hither and thither, they killed the earl's men. So many were killed that every street was covered with blood, and filled with bodies. The blood that flowed in the streets was frozen by the bitter January winds.

"The earl himself held out in a house near Palace Green so the rebels set it on fire. The flaming sparks, flying upwards, caught the western tower of the Cathedral. The people knelt down and begged St. Cuthbert to save his church from burning; and immediately a wind arose from the east which drove the flames backwards from the church.

"The house, however, which had caught fire, continued to blaze; and of those persons who were within it some were burnt, some were slaughtered as soon as they stepped outside. The earl was put to death along with all of his followers, save one, who escaped wounded."

Five foul facts about the Conqueror's revenge

1. The Normans were fine soldiers but were helpless in the narrow Durham streets. As they fought the rebels who attacked from outside, the Durham people picked up knives and sickles and attacked them from the inside, too. The Durham people had already suffered Norman bullying - Cumyn had thrown the abbot out of his house on Palace Green, the same house that was later burned by the rebels. The people of Durham were in no mood to show any mercy. Neither was William the Conqueror when he heard about the massacre.

2. William didn't return at once. He waited till September. His avenging force reached Northallerton, north of York ... then were turned back by a miracle (the Durham people said.). The Norman army marched into a thick fog (sent by St. Cuthbert probably). They panicked and turned back. Durham was saved.

But the truth is an invading Danish army landed on the Yorkshire coast – the Normans turned back to deal with the invaders first.

Durham was not saved for long.

3. The monks in Durham dug up Cuthbert – again – to carry him to the safety of Lindisfarne. When they reached the coast at Lindisfarne they couldn't find a boat to carry them across. As they stood there, the water level fell and the monks were able to carry the coffin over the sand to the monastery on Lindisfarne. Another miracle. That's what they believed. But we know it was just the tide going out and leaving a path, the way it does twice every day. While the monks saved Cuthbert their bishop saved all the Cathedral's treasure – he ran away with it. Just in time. The Danish invaders had been driven back. The Normans were coming.

4. William didn't just want to defeat the North – he wanted to destroy it. Every building his soldiers came across was burned. Every animal was killed so there was nothing left for the people to eat. Every man and boy they found was hacked to death – their corpses were left to rot by the side of the roads. The starving survivors were so desperate they ate the corpses to stay alive. William's ruthless revenge was known as "The Harrying of the North".

5. The North was like a desert. The towns and villages were still struggling to recover twenty years later. The North certainly didn't revolt again. The Conqueror's cruelty worked. Yet there's a curious story that, nearly twenty years after the destruction, William said he was sorry it had happened.

CHAPTER 6

COOL CASTLE

Durham Castle courtyard

On this spot ... the ghostly Grey Lady walks.

The story goes that one of Durham's Prince Bishops had a wife who came to a nasty end. One evening she was standing at the top of the Castle's Black Staircase when she fell crashing to a horribly tangled and mangled death.

Since then her ghostly form has haunted the castle. But ghosts only haunt a place when they are unable to settle till something on earth has been settled. So what is the Grey Lady so unhappy about?

Perhaps she was pushed and she is seeking justice. The Grey Lady's isn't the only dreadful death to happen around the castle, of course. It ought to be haunted by dozens of other suffering souls.

The story of Malcolm's misery

The castle was built by the Normans to control the troublesome Durham people - and to keep out the even more troublesome Scots.

Malcolm III was king of the Scots when William the Conqueror invaded England and harried the North to destruction. Malcolm saw the chance to grab the North while there was so much confusion.

The Scots invaded time and again.

Fifth time unlucky - he didn't get as far as Durham when he was murdered by his "sworn brother". Don't feel too sorry for him - he'd won the throne by murdering that nice King Macbeth.

And even if he'd reached Durham that fifth time he could have been defeated. The Durham people were used to beating back the Scots. King Duncan's Scots had been there in 1039 - and failed again.

Back in 1006 King Malcolm II was defeated at Durham and thousands of Scots died.

The heads of the dead Scottish soldiers were cut off and put on display round the walls of Durham City. But some women of Durham offered to comb the hair of the dead Scots heads if the Scottish relatives paid them. Gruesome.

Those Durham walls had held out - but a castle would be better and so it was built. Of course, the bishops who ruled Durham - the Prince Bishops - needed somewhere to live in safety and the Castle made a grand palace.

Who were these Prince Bishops?

Five fantastic facts about peculiar Prince Bishops

The Normans worried that northern princes might become too powerful and threaten the king. So the king made his bishops into northern princes. Bishops weren't supposed to marry and have children so no ruling "family" of princes could grow in the North. They were Prince Bishops. A good idea - yet they never had Prince Bishops anywhere else but Durham.

1. **William of St. Carileph** - 1081 - 1096. Accused of plotting against the King. He was packed off to Normandy in exile. The bishop was lucky. The leader of the plot - Bishop Odo - was thrown into jail. The new king, William II, forgave William of St. Carileph, and he returned. He decided Durham should have a magnificent cathedral and flattened Cuthbert's little wooden church to build it.

2. **Ranulf Flambard** - 1099 - 1128. Ranulf was a great supporter of William II but the king died after a mysterious "accident" with an arrow. The new king, Henry I, threw Bishop Ranulf into the Tower of London. He escaped but made his peace with Henry and returned. He saw Cuthbert's bones moved into the new cathedral in 1104.

3. **Hugh Pudsey (de Puiset)** - 1153 - 1195. Not very religious, but the nephew of King Stephen, so he got the job. He used the job to make his fortune. He gave King Richard the Lionheart money to go on the Crusades and Richard gave him Northumberland in return.

4. **Antony Bek** - 1284 - 1310. So powerful his own servant wrote: "There are two kings in England, the one in London who wears a crown and the Bishop of Durham who wears a Bishop's mitre [hat]". In fact Bek did hold the title "king" for four years when he became "King of the Isle of Man". He rode at the head of a Durham army that invaded Scotland. That would suit the battling bishop because he quarrelled with just about everyone including King Edward I - the king took Bek's power from him three times, but gave it back every time.

5. **Thomas Wolsey** - 1523 - 1529. Famous minister of King Henry VIII who came close to becoming Pope. He made a fortune from being bishop of Durham - but never ever visited the place. (None of the Tudor monarchs got any further north than York.) He became too powerful so Henry had him arrested. Lucky Wolsey died before he went to the Tower of London for the chop.

CHAPTER 7

BORDER BOTHER

The Cathedral tower

On this spot ... in 1346 many of the monks of Durham were able to watch the Battle of Neville's Cross. They climbed the steps to pray that the Scots would lose.

The Scots took with them a piece of wood - said to be from the cross that Jesus died on.

So both sides were hoping God was with them - that day he was with the English. The monks' prayers were answered and the Scots invaders defeated - again.

The story of David's defeat

In the autumn of 1346 David, King of Scotland gathered one of the most powerful armies which had ever crossed the border - he knew English King Edward was away in France with his best knights. Devious David decided it would be a good time to catch the English when they were weak.

The Scots arrived at Bearpark, three miles west of Durham. They began looting the country around Durham instead of attacking the city while they had the chance. David didn't even bother having lookouts to warn him of an English attack. The northern nobles had gathered an army of 16,000 men.

On 17 October the armies met on the Red-hills, a piece of rough ground near the Wear.

The Scots knights drove the English archers back and looked like winning but English knight, Edward Baliol, led a powerful charge on the Scots forces and chased them from the battlefield.

When the battle was as good as lost, a band of Scots knights formed themselves around their king, and fought till only eighty of them survived. It also gave their king the chance to get away.

David, after receiving two arrow wounds, escaped from the battlefield in spite

of several attempts to take him captive. But he was caught later, hiding under a bridge.

Out of an army of 30,000 Scots 15,000 were left dead on the field, whilst the English lost very few.

Five fantastic facts about Neville's Cross

Saint Cuthbert had been dead for almost 660 years when the Battle of Neville's Cross was fought. Yet the people of Durham believed he'd helped them win.

1. It is said that, as David approached Durham, he had a dream in which he was warned not to invade St. Cuthbert's holy territory. Ignoring this warning, David continued his advance.

The night before the battle St. Cuthbert appeared in a dream to Prior Fossor of Durham. Cuthbert said, "Take the holy cloth that was found in my coffin in 1104, fasten it to a spear and carry it as a banner to the battlefield."

Early the following day, the Prior took this holy relic to a place just a few hundred metres from the two armies. There, he and the monks raised the holy cloth so the fighting men on both sides could see it. It seems to have worked.

2. King David himself managed to escape. But legend says that, while hiding under a bridge over the nearby River Browney, David's reflection was spotted in the water by a group of English soldiers that were out searching for him. David was forced to surrender to John Copeland, a Northumbrian squire, but not before David had punched John in the mouth with his armoured fist and knocked out the young man's teeth. Later, King Edward III ordered Copeland to bring the Scots king to Calais and hand him over.

3. Edward then rewarded Copeland with a knighthood and a handsome lump of money - a sort of very rich tooth fairy. King David was brought back to England and imprisoned in the Tower of London. After eleven years in the Tower, he was released in return for a ransom of 100,000 marks - worth about £15 million today.

4. The Battle of Neville's Cross gets its name from a stone cross that Lord Neville paid to have put up on the battlefield to remember this great victory. There had been a cross there before and Neville replaced it with his. Redhills Lane is still there today and got its name because the hill ran red with the blood of the Scottish soldiers.

5. The monastery at Durham was closed by Henry VIII. St. Cuthbert's holy cloth fell into the hands of Dean Whittingham whose wife, Katherine, burned it on her fire. It was a "relic" and the Tudors thought that sort of thing was little better than witchcraft. The Scots "relic" - the wood from Jesus' cross - was captured by the English, and was placed in Durham Cathedral. It disappeared around the same time as Cuthbert's cloth.

CHAPTER 8

ROWDY REBELS

Northgate

On this spot ... an army of rebels marched on the Cathedral. But this wasn't a people's rebellion like the one against William the Conqueror. This was a rebellion led by the great lords of the North. Durham was just a stopping place on their way to London. There they would overthrow Queen Elizabeth I and take over England.

If they had succeeded then England could have been ruled by Northerners. It was a close thing and this spot saw the menacing marchers heading towards the Cathedral.

What was their problem?

The story of the battered Bibles

There were five Tudor monarchs from 1485 to 1603 and not one of them bothered to visit Durham. They sat in London and passed their laws while Durham people had no say. Even a bishop of Durham, Cardinal Wolsey, took the riches of Durham but didn't make the effort to visit and say thanks.

So it's no wonder that rebellions started in the North. Henry VIII got rid of the Catholic religion and the monasteries - the main rebellion (called "The

dph324-93

Pilgrimage of Grace") came from the North.

Then, in 1569, Henry's daughter, Elizabeth I, faced an even more serious revolt from the lords in the North – called (of course) The Northern Rebellion.

The Earl of Northumberland was behaving like a Catholic. Elizabeth ordered him to come to London to go on trial. Sensible Northumberland said, "I'd like to – but I'm too busy. Sorry."

HOORAY!! NOT ONLY HAVE I ESCAPED BUT I'VE ALSO INVENTED THE PARACHUTE!!

But the rebel Duke did march south with an army – Elizabeth sent her army north to meet him – but the queen's army stopped at York.

These rebels wanted to worship in the old Catholic way and where better to do it than Durham Cathedral? On 13 November 1,500 of the Earl of Northumberland's rebels marched through Northgate and over Palace Green. They tore and trampled the English Bibles, then went on to hold a service in Durham Cathedral.

They smashed the tables where the Protestant services were held. They would have smashed the priests ... but they had wisely run away before the rebels arrived.

But the rebels got very little support. After the Durham attack they soon fled or went home as Elizabeth's army advanced.

The Earl of Northumberland was executed in York.

Five foul facts about northern rebel nastiness

1. After raiding Durham the rebels turned to attack Barnard Castle. Castle commander, Sir George Bowes, barred the gates, of course. Some people inside Barnard Castle wanted to join the rebels but they couldn't get out through the

locked gates. If they wanted to escape they had to jump over the walls instead. Dangerous. Sir George Bowes, wrote: "In one day the castle lost 226 soldiers, though 35 of these broke their necks, legs or arms in leaping."

2. The Barnard Castle jumpers who survived may have wished they hadn't. Twenty of them were caught and executed by avenging Elizabeth's army. As Elizabeth's army marched north they stole the food they needed to survive. The peasants of the North went hungry that winter - just as northern peasants had when William the conqueror "harried" the North 500 years before. The revolt wasn't their fault but they suffered even if they loved the Tudor queen.

3. When Elizabeth decided to take her revenge she hanged many of the people who had supported the rebels. Sir George Bowes of Barnard Castle wrote cheerfully: "Sixty-six persons suffered death at Durham. In sixty miles, from Wetherby to Newcastle, it is said, there was hardly a village which did not see the execution of some of the foolish rebels."

4. A total of 917 rebels were captured and brought to trial. Of the 917 19 were described as "gentlemen" - the rest were poorer people. Of the 917 228 were executed. But how many of the "gentlemen" were hanged? After all, it was a revolt of the lords and the poor had simply tagged along. Not one of the "gentlemen" dangled from the end of a rope. The Earl of Northumberland was beheaded.

5. One of Elizabeth's spies wrote to her: "The common people are saying that the poor are ruined or executed but the gentlemen and the rich escape." As usual it was the ordinary people who suffered the most when the Tudors' lost their temper.

CHAPTER 9

DEADLY DURHAM

Fleshergate - where Saddler Street meets the Market Place

On this spot ... you could see animals slaughtered for sale in the shops. A report said: "There are three butchers' shops fronting the street in which the animals are slaughtered, there being no public slaughter-house nor places behind the shops for such purpose."

It was no wonder that disease spread so easily through the narrow streets.

The Market Place is mostly built over the graveyard of St Nicholas's Church and you can still find disease victims there. It's not unusual for bones to be uncovered when workers dig up the cobbles. In 1994 electric cables were laid to the Tourism office and four skeletons were uncovered. One was of a child.

The story of dirty Durham

Elizabeth I was the last of the Tudors. The Stuarts took the place of the Tudors until Charles I was thrown off the throne by Oliver Cromwell's Roundheads. The Roundheads left Charles I with no head and ran the country until Charles II took the throne again in 1660. But some things didn't change.

Death and disease still made Durham a dangerous place to live. Especially when plagues swept through the town. The narrow streets and back alleys meant there was no escape.

The plague was carried by fleas that lived on rats.

The fleas bit the rats to suck their blood and infected the rats.

The rats died.

The fleas didn't like cold rat blood so they looked for another animal to jump on. If that animal was a human then the human would be infected and probably die a painful death.

Plague victims sweated and swelled - they also *smelled* dreadful. They were usually dead within a week.

Durham escaped the Great Plague of 1665 but many of the corpses still under Durham Market Place must have been victims of other diseases that came from the filth.

The River Wear was an open sewer where all the filth of the town was tipped. As usual the poor lived in the worst conditions of dirt and disease. And the customs of the time didn't help ...

Five foul facts about plague, powder and pews

1. If you wanted to avoid the plague then there was a custom for families to hire a "sin-eater." This was a poor person who was given a loaf of bread to eat and a beer to drink ... while standing over the corpse. The idea was the dead person's sins would enter the bread and be eaten by the poor person - their ghost could then get into heaven.

DON'T TELL ME...THERE'S SOMETHING DIFFERENT ABOUT YOU! I KNOW! YOU'VE DONE YOUR HAIR DIFFERENTLY?

2. Getting married in St. Nicholas's Church would be too expensive for some poor couples. Some went to a wandering "priest" who made money by performing marriage ceremonies for couples. These fake clergymen called themselves Strollers' Priests. The marriage was made by the bride and groom shaking hands ... over the corpse of a dead horse.

3. Church services must have been pretty boring anyway. A lot of gunpowder was needed in Oliver Cromwell's civil war against Charles. To make gunpowder the army needed "saltpetre". This was made from bird-droppings and human urine. Cromwell's officers had the right to dig these from hen-houses and toilets. In 1638 "Saltpetre men" tried to get permission to go into churches like St Nicholas's to collect human urine that had soaked into the pews. They said, "Women pee in their seats which causes excellent saltpetre." (It must have been those long, long, long sermons.)

4. The disgusting, slaughtering butchers' shops in Fleshergate would be busy at Christmas - but not selling turkeys. They would be selling the ingredients for Christmas puddings. You probably enjoy the candied peel, raisins, sugar and spices in modern Christmas puddings. So did the Stuarts. They were all in the Stuart pudding ... along with chopped cow's tongue and chicken.

5. Dig beneath the Market Place and you will find more than bones - you will find some of the odd things people were buried with in the 1600s and 1700s. You may find:
   - a coin (to pay St. Peter at the gates of heaven).
   - a candle (to light the way to heaven).
   - a ten-centimetre layer of bran cereal on the bottom of the coffin (for comfort).

CHAPTER 10
DURHAM'S DICK WHITTINGTON

Silver Street

On this spot ... Durham's "Dick Whittington" lived. The man was Sir John Duck, and Duck (like Dick) arrived as a poor man and ended his life rich and a famous mayor. His home was on Silver Street. Silver Street is still there today but sadly you can't see Duck's house today because it was demolished in 1963.

Silver Street may have got its name because that's where silver coins were made in the Middle Ages. It was certainly the place where John Duck earned himself a lot of silver.

The story of Duck's delight

It's a mystery. Where did young John Duck come from? No one knows.

But they say young John arrived in Durham in 1655 with a dream. A dream of becoming a butcher's apprentice.

The young man tramped around every butcher in Durham but at each shop the answer was the same. "We don't know you – who you are or where you're from. We know nothing about your family. We don't give jobs to strangers. It will cost you gold to be an apprentice."

The truth may be that they suspected John Duck could have been one of those dreadful people – a Scot. And it was against the guild law to offer a job to a Scot in those days.

As young Duck was wandering by the riverside in Durham and about to turn his back on Durham and leave, suddenly a passing raven dropped a coin of gold at his feet. The boy was so encouraged he decided to try just one last shop. Clutching his lucky gold coin he walked into the shop of John Heslop.

Like all the others Heslop was about to turn Duck down when the butcher's daughter, Anne, took pity on the weary and ragged boy. "Give him a job, father," she

35

asked quietly. John Heslop could never refuse his daughter. Duck got the job ... and, of course, he also got the girl.

He married her the same year. With Anne's help (and her father's money that they inherited) Duck went on to become one of the richest men in Durham. He owned both land and collieries in the area.

In 1680 he became the mayor of Durham. In 1686 he became a baronet - Sir John Duck of Haswell on the Hill.

He died in 1691.

The story of Duck and Dick and chicks

1. Was John Duck a Scot? A 1527 law said:

"Every apprentice must serve seven years and pay at his entrance a pound of wax. The masters must take no Scotsmen as apprentices or give work to any. The fine for doing so is forty shillings."

In the same year one craft guild in Newcastle passed a rule that said:

"Any apprentice who calls another apprentice 'Scot' shall be fined six shillings and eight pence."

Just the word "Scot" was an insult. When Duck arrived in Durham, 130 years later, there was still a great distrust of Scots.

2. The late 1600s were a time of pirates and highwaymen. A time when the poor really could make a fortune - with a bit of luck ... and maybe a bit of law-breaking. There are rumours that Sir John Duck made some of his fortune by illegal means. Beef for the butcher shop was expensive to buy from the farmers. But crafty John bought stolen cattle for half the price and sold them. That way he made an even bigger profit. That could be a lie, made up by jealous rivals, but it could explain his success.

3. Of course the story of cattle-stealing could be someone getting mixed up with an even more famous butcher's apprentice - Dick Turpin. Around 1720 Dick Turpin was apprentice to a butcher in Whitechapel, a village on the edge of London in those days. Turpin decided to make extra money by stealing two cows that he would kill and sell in the butcher shop. But clumsy Turpin was caught and had to flee for his life. That was why he became a highwayman. If Dick had got away with it he may have ended up rich as Duck.

4. Butchers like Duck didn't have fridges in Stuart times (1603 - 1714) but they did know that freezing kept meat fresh. Sir Francis Bacon of London noticed how fresh grass was under the snow. He decided to see if snow would keep dead meat fresh. He caught a chicken, killed it and stuffed it with snow. The chicken stayed fresh. Sir Francis didn't - the snow gave him a chill that killed him. The chicken went on to haunt Pond Square in London and was last seen in 1970.

5. Chickens had a hard time in those days. In 1758 an advert for a fair in north Durham said:

"A man will eat a cockerel alive, feathers, entrails and all."

CHAPTER 11

KING COAL

Market Place

On this spot ... is the statue to Lord Londonderry. It was erected in 1861, seven years after he died. The statue was designed by Signor Monti, and made using latest electromagnetic techniques. A legend says the Durham Council were terrifically proud of their statue and claimed it was perfect. Everyone who came to see it agreed. But then a blind man asked to examine it. He ran his hands over every inch of the statue and noticed something everyone else had missed. Londonderry's horse has no tongue.

It was said that the sculptor, Signor Raphael Monti (1818-1881), killed himself when he heard the news. He *didn't*.

And how did the blind man manage to reach the horse's mouth? It's pretty high up.

The statue looks grand today but in the past it stood above the Market Place's underground toilets. (They were closed in 1975.)

The story of the mine millionaire

Charles William Stewart (1778-1854), Lord Londonderry, started his adult life as a soldier. His nickname was "Fighting Charlie"

for his army adventures around Europe. But he married the wealthy Lady Frances Anne Vane-Tempest and returned to look after her Durham coal fields ... and her money.

The Durham coal was shipped from Londonderry's mines, down the River Wear, to Sunderland and loaded onto the coal ships. That cost his lordship money - £10,000 a year - so he came up with a great scheme. He'd turn wild, smuggler-infested village of Seaham into a harbour of his own. Then he'd build a railway to carry his coal to his new harbour.

Some people said he was mad to attempt it. But after seven years he finally found enough people to lend him the money to carry out his dream. A song of the time had the chorus:

"May we live to see the day
When ships are laid at anchor
Safe in Seaham's bay."

In 1828 the foundation stone of the harbour was laid. Londonderry had brought wealth to Durham City so the statue was erected in his memory. Of course Londonderry brought a lot more wealth to himself and his family.

In 1822 the workers were earning a few pounds a year for a life of dirty and dangerous work. In that year Lord Londonderry's Penshaw and Rainton Collieries earned him £61,364.

Meanwhile the men, women and children who did the work suffered in the misery of the mines. What a shame there isn't room for a statue to some of them.

Five foul facts about pit perils

1. An 1842 report said: "Pit managers say they take children to work in the pits from the age of nine. Unfortunately there is proof that children go down into many of the pits at a much earlier age. In some cases as early as between five and six." The pit managers blamed the parents who pestered them to take young children as workers.

2. Whatever the age the work was hard. The report went on: "In some pits the boys do not start work until 5a.m. and there are some pits where it is 6a.m. But whatever time they start they have to work for twelve hours. In talking with the miners and boys I never found one of them complain of the early hour at which they went to work." Most wouldn't dare complain, of course. They worked - or they starved.

3. The work wasn't hard but it was miserable. "His place of work is inside one of

the doors called trap-doors. This door must be opened whenever men or boys, with or without carriages, wish to pass through. He seats himself in a little hole, about the size of a common fireplace, and with the string in his hand; and all his work is to pull his string when he has to open the door, and when man or boy has passed through, then allow the door to shut of itself...

"He sits alone with no one to talk to him; for in the pit the whole of the people are as busy as if they were in a sea-fight ... he himself has no light. His hours...are passed in total darkness."

4. And in the darkness there are other uncomfortable things: "That the air of the pit does not destroy all life. Horses thrive well, and so do asses, if the pit be not too warm. Midges are in millions. Wood-lice are common, so are insects called forty-legs; and beetles are found in all parts of the pit." There's a nice bit of company as you sit in the dark.

5. If the trapper boys failed to open a door on time they would be whipped by the miners. Many fell asleep and woke up to a thrashing. Some fell asleep across the underground railway line. If a truck came along they could lose a leg, or lose their life. James Morrow was seven years old when he first worked in a mine. On his first day he fell asleep and a truck sliced off his leg. James was fitted with a wooden leg and returned to his job three months later. Before he was nine unlucky James was killed when a roof collapsed on him.

CHAPTER 12

PITIFUL PRISONERS

Elvet Bridge

On this spot ... was the entrance to the old jail.

The river's edge was a good place for a jail in the early 1800s. The prisoners could be put on a boat and taken down the river to the sea ports. From there they would suffer the horrible fate of "transportation" to Australia.

If they survived the journey they faced years of hard labour in criminal gangs.

The transported criminals lived a savage life. The first convicts arrived in Tasmania in 1802. There were 20,000 native Tasmanians on the island at the time. Just seventy four years later the last native Tasmanian died.

A whole nation had been wiped out by the brutal British convicts - including some from Durham's old jail.

The story of the pitiful piper

Go down the steps at the end of Elvet Bridge. Go to the water's edge. That's the spot where the old jail opened onto the river.

Go at a quiet time and you may just hear the heartbreaking moan of bagpipes. If you do hear them then you'll know you are hearing a ghost.

It's the ghost of an old gypsy who was arrested in 1803. He'd had a long and wicked career as a horse thief and at last the Durham magistrates had had enough of him. They wouldn't lock him up, this time. They sentenced him to transportation.

He was an old man. His health was failing. He would never survive the three-month journey. The sentence was as good as a sentence to death. A slow, miserable death on board a stinking, rat-infested ship.

But the old horse thief never set foot on that ship. He was too weak to travel so he was kept in old Durham jail till he recovered. A year in the jail turned into two, then three. After seven years the Prince of Wales heard about the old man's suffering. Old King George, the Prince's father, was too mad to give a royal pardon. The Prince of Wales himself sent the pardon north from London.

It was a three day ride over rutted and muddy roads for the messenger. At last he reached Durham Jail. "Take me to the governor of the jail." he demanded. "I come from the Prince."

"The governor is busy," he was told. "He's arranging the funeral of an old gypsy horse thief. He died just an hour ago."

Five filthy facts about transportation

1. In the early 1800s there were over 200 crimes that could be punished with the death sentence. In 1805 George Ainsley of Durham was sentenced to death for breaking in to a house and was sentenced to hang for it. But many judges were not happy about hanging a man for such a crime. They were delighted that they could "transport" a man, woman or child criminal instead. Ainsley's sentence was changed. He was given fourteen years in Australia instead of a noose.

2. Ainsley was lucky to be sent in 1805. The worst Australian convict master was Major Joseph Foveaux who was in charge from 1800 to 1804. He flogged prisoners till their bones showed through the torn flesh then threw salt water over the wounds and sent the men straight back to work. He had leg irons made small so they cut into the ankles and he had a half-flooded punishment cell. If the prisoner dared to fall asleep he'd drown.

3. Durham records seemed to show the judges had a choice between seven years or fourteen years - nothing more, nothing less or nothing between. So Gordon Alexander was given seven years for stealing a pair of candlesticks in 1805 while

Christopher Scorton got fourteen years for stealing a horse. Barbara Oliver got fourteen years for forging bank notes in 1816 while highwayman Christopher Humble Junior got just seven years a short while before her.

4. When criminals returned from Australia they were not usually better people – but they were often better criminals. They learned lots of new tricks from the other convicts. Any who escaped a seven year sentence and returned home would be sent back for fourteen years. Anyone escaping a second time was hanged.

In fact very few convicts returned to Britain. They couldn't afford the fare. Many couldn't face the dreadful journey.

5. The oldest convict to go from Britain was eighty-two-year-old Dorothy Handland. She survived the trip but hanged herself from a gum tree when she arrived. John Hudson stole some clothes and a gun and became the youngest person to be transported. He was nine years old. Transportation was ended in 1868.

CHAPTER 13

PRISON PAIN

Durham Jail Green

On this spot ... criminals were executed in public.

In 1868 public hanging was stopped but the hangings still went on behind those grim, grey walls. Britain's greatest Victorian serial killer, Mary Ann Cotton was hanged there in 1873. Just two years later Elizabeth Pearson poisoned her uncle and was found guilty. She was put in Mary Ann Cotton's death cell and suffered the same end. Even today some of Britain's most infamous criminals live behind bars in there.

The story of Murdering Mary

Mary Ann Cotton was born just a few miles east of Durham City but moved around a lot ... and that was how she managed to murder at least fifteen people (maybe twenty) and not be caught for twenty years.

She was a lively and beautiful young woman but hated being tied down by husbands and babies. She soon tired of them and learned that arsenic poison would kill them - slowly and painfully.

The doctors all said the victims had stomach problems. Mary's neighbours gave her sympathy. The insurance companies paid her for her dead husband and she moved on ... again ... and again.

At last she arrived in West Auckland in south-west Durham. Here her last husband, her new boyfriend and three children all died in a few months and the police became suspicious. The body of seven-year-old Charles Edward Cotton was examined and the doctor said the victim could have died of a stomach problem. She was released - but stayed around to raise some money by selling her furniture. She should have taken the chance to escape.

HOW'S ABOUT A LOVELY CUP OF TEA, PET?

The day after her release the local newspapers looked back over her life and published details of some of the other "stomach problem" victims who had died in Mary Ann's homes.

Charles Edward's corpse was examined a second time. This time the doctor found the arsenic.

Mary Ann Cotton was sentenced to death.

She was hanged in Durham jail in 1873. Mary Ann Cotton died saying she was innocent.

Five foul facts about Durham death-bringers

1. If Mary Ann Cotton murdered twelve or more children, as they say, then children of Durham took a curious revenge. They made up a skipping song about her. It was still being sung a hundred years after her execution. The oddly gruesome words go ...
Mary Ann Cotton, she's dead and she's rotten,
She lies on her bed with her eyes wide open.
Sing, sing. What shall I sing?
Mary Ann Cotton is tied up with string.
Where, where? Up in the air,
Selling black puddings a penny a pair.

2. Just two years after Mary Ann Cotton was executed *The Times* newspaper was shocked to report that *four* people were in Durham jail waiting to be executed. The newspaper was especially shocked by the case of Elizabeth Pearson who poisoned her seventy-four-year-old uncle for a few "miserable" pieces of his furniture. She had a respectable husband and five children. Elizabeth, the report went on, wept as she was led away to her cell but never admitted the crime and refused to talk about it. She was hanged. Elizabeth Pearson was twenty-eight-years-old.

3. Elizabeth Pearson was hanged at the same time as two other Durham killers. Crowds gathered on the green outside the jail. At quarter to eight the Cathedral bell began to ring. The executions were carried out at eight and there was a signal that they'd been carried out. A black flag was raised above the prison.

4. A local newspaper complained about the three hangings inside the jail. *The Northern Daily Express* reporter said that the whole idea of executing people was to put people off murder. The murderer should be taken through the streets of the city and hanged in front of the jail where everyone could see them. That was how they did it until ten years before. Since they'd started hanging people "in secret" ten years ago there had been lots more murders and twelve executions. It was time to go back to public hanging. The reporter never got his wish.

5. Michael Gilligan was hanged alongside Elizabeth Pearson. He'd been one of a gang of seven who beat a man to death. Six escaped death sentence but Gilligan, aged twenty two, was hanged. He said it was because he was Irish – and he could have been right.

CHAPTER 14

WORMY WEAR

The Riverside

On this spot ... the River Wear flows out of Durham City towards the sea. And the river is the real reason for Durham being the place it is. The river carved its way round the rock where the Cathedral and Castle stand today – the river made it a perfect place to build a castle.

The river also became the place of Durham's greatest legend – the legend of the Lambton Worm.

The story of the Wicked Worm

Young John Lambton was a wicked lad. When he should have been in church he went fishing in the Wear, just ten miles down from Durham. The devil himself fastened himself onto John's line in the form of an ugly worm. John took one look at the creature and threw it down a nearby well.

Young John forgot about the creature in the well and left Durham to fight in the

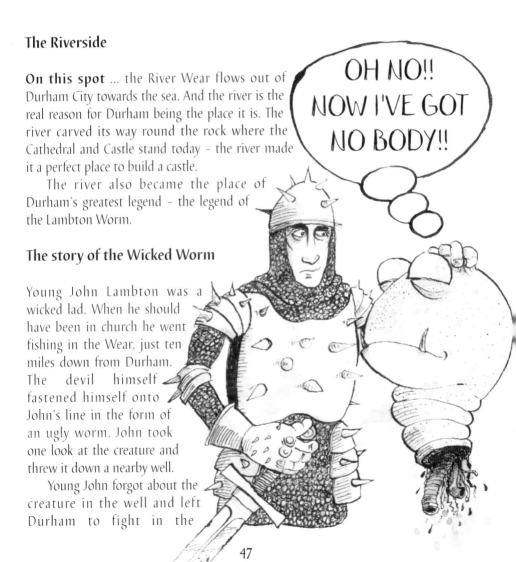

OH NO!! NOW I'VE GOT NO BODY!!

Crusades. Meanwhile the Lambton Worm grew and escaped from the well. It ate everything in sight and grew to a monstrous size.

The local people tried to kill it but the worm managed to join itself together with its magical power.

John returned and he too failed to cut the monster in half. Then he went to the local wise woman who told him how to defeat the evil worm. In return he had to promise to kill the first thing he saw after the battle.

John followed her advice and had a suit of armour made, spiked with sword and spear points. Then he walked into the river Wear and challenged the worm to fight. The Worm circled him and tried to crush him – but cut itself to pieces on the sharp armour. Because it was in the river the pieces were washed away before they could join back on again. The shredded worm was dead.

John stepped out of the river to kill the first living thing he saw – it was supposed to be an old hunting hound, specially released for the purpose. But the hound got lost and the first thing John saw was ... his own father. "I can't kill you, Father," he sighed.

And so the curse fell on the Lambton family – no lord of Lambton died in his bed for seven generations.

All because John Lambton went fishing in the Wear on a Sunday.

Five fascinating facts about Wear worms

1. Did John Lambton's curse really exist? A John Lambton, "Knight of Rhodes", is mentioned in his mother's will of 1442. This is probably the worm-slayer. Some historians have claimed that seven generations of Lambtons did indeed die out of their beds - from coach accidents to death on the battlefield. But then, many people did die violently in the Middle Ages.

2. Did the Worm exist? Yes ... sort of. Imagine the worm isn't a creature but a silvery line of Scottish raiders who snaked their way down to the Wear valley while the lord was away. They raided the estates, killing and driving off the stock, till the terrified people were starving. The Scots camped in a circle around a hill - like a worm - so no matter where their line was attacked they could join back up and repel the attackers. John came back from war and used a sensible tactic. He stood at the far side of the Wear and challenged the Scots to come and get him. As they struggled across the river John's forces attacked them – this time the Scots line couldn't join back up and they were washed away to their deaths – like a worm. The explanation fits most of the facts.

48

3. What about the famous song, "The Lambton Worm"? It's not an ancient folk song. It's a Victorian music hall song less than 150 years old. And it gets some facts wrong. The worm in the song wrapped itself "ten times round Penshaw Hill" - a huge hill needing a worm about five miles long. The legend says it was wrapped around "Worm Hill" - a small hummock on the opposite bank of the Wear.

4. Will the Worm ever return? Maybe it did in 1569. A report in a parish register says:

"On the 11th day of June an Italian brought into the City of Durham a very great strange and monstrous serpent, sixteen feet in length, and eleven times greater than a great horse. It had been taken and killed in Ethiopia. But before it was killed, it had devoured more than 1,000 persons and also eaten a whole country."
Some worm. Some story.

5. Where did the legend come from? Maybe an old tale going back to where we started - with St. Cuthbert. The story goes, an idle and wicked shepherd called Osulf went to sleep in a field and woke to find a serpent was twisted round his neck. He grabbed it in his hand, and dashed it to the ground, but it twined itself round his neck a second time. It didn't matter if he threw the snake into the fire, or the water, or on the ground, it always returned to his neck. Sometimes he took a sword and cut it into pieces; but it was soon back round his neck. And at first it was a very little snake, but it gradually grew larger and larger. In desperation he fled to the Cathedral and prayed for St Cuthbert's help. The serpent fell away as he entered the door. Osulf prayed three days and nights and was saved.

No matter where you turn in Durham you come back to Cuthbert and his Cathedral. Remember to ask for his help if you ever meet an ugly worm ....

SOURCES

A Coffin and a cow

For the legend of the Dun Cow see:
J.T. Fowler ed., *Rites of Durham, being a description or brief declaration of all the ancient Monuments, Rites, and customs belonging or being within the Monastical Church of Durham before the Suppression, written 1593.* Surtees Society, 1903, pages 66,71,74

Saints and Smiths

For the story of the Uncorrupted Corpse see:
J.T. Fowler ed., *Rites of Durham, being a description or brief declaration of all the ancient Monuments, Rites, and customs belonging or being within the Monastical Church of Durham before the Suppression, written 1593.* Surtees Society, 1903, page 102

For the tale of William the Conqueror and St. Cuthbert see:
Simeon of Durham A history of the Church of Durham, Translated by Joseph Stevenson, Facsimile reprinted 1988, Llanerch Enterprises, page 75

For the opening of Cuthbert's tomb in 1827 and its examination in 1899 see:
William Page ed., *The Victory County History of Durham, Volume I,* pages 241-254

Bede's Bones

For the story of Bede's bones see:
Simeon of Durham A history of the Church of Durham, Translated by Joseph Stevenson, Facsimile reprinted 1988, Llanerch Enterprises, pages 62-63

Wicked Women

For the building of the Galilee Chapel see:
J.T. Fowler ed., *Rites of Durham, being a description or brief declaration of all the ancient Monuments, Rites, and customs belonging or being within the Monastical Church of Durham before the Suppression, written 1593.* Surtees Society, 1903, page 43

The tale of Sungeova
Simeon of Durham A history of the Church of Durham, Translated by Joseph Stevenson, Facsimile reprinted 1988, Llanerch Enterprises, page 42

Queen Philippa and St Cuthbert
John Sykes, *Historical Register of Remarkable Events, volume 1,* page 41

Fire and Fury

The murder of Robert Cumyn
John Sykes, *Historical Register of Remarkable Events, volume 1,* page 11

Simeon of Durham A history of the Church of Durham, Translated by Joseph Stevenson, Facsimile reprinted 1988, Llanerch Enterprises, page 69-70

Border Bother

John Sykes, *Historical Register of Remarkable Events, volume 1,* page 44-47

Durham County Council, *The Battle of Neville's Cross,* 1996

Rowdy Rebels

The Northern Rebellion, 1569
John Sykes, *Historical Register of Remarkable Events, volume 1*, page 77-78

William Fordyce, *The History of the Antiquities of Durham, Volume 1*, page 67 (1855)

Sir Cuthbert Sharp, *Memorials of the Rebellion of the Earls of Northumberland and Westmoreland* (published 1840, reprinted in 1975 as *The Rising in the North The 1569 Rebellion*), selected pages 41-42, 133

Deadly Durham

Report to the Public Board of Health, on a preliminary enquiry into the sewerage, Drainage, and Supply of Water, and the sanitary condition of the Inhabitants of the Borough of Durham, 1849 (Reprinted as Durham 1849, Durham County Local History Society)

Durham St. Nicholas burial registers deposited in Durham Record Office (reference EP/Du.SN1/2)

Emery, Langston and Leyland, *St. Nicholas' Church and Cemetry, Durham City*, in *Durham Archaeological Journal 13*, 1997, page 70

King Coal

The *records of the Londonderry Family* are deposited in the Durham Record Office (DRO)

Children in the Pits

Report by James Mitchell, LL.D., on the *Employment of Children and Young Persons in the Mines of the South Durham Coalfield, betweene the Weare and the Tees; and on the State, Condition, and Treatment of such Children and Young Persons.* 1842. DRO ref: G249

Pitiful Prisoners

Transportees from Durham:
Criminal register Indexes, 1805-1816 Volume 10. Cumberland, Westmorland, Northumberland Durham (PRO Class HO 27). Indexed by Stuart Tamblin.

Prison pain

Execution of Elizabeth Pearson and other, 1875
Durham Advertiser, July and August 1875

Coroners reports, DRO ref: COR/C/2/348

Wormy Wear

Monster serpent in Durham
Durham St. Nicholas register of baptisms, marriages and burials, 1540-1705, Christenings, 1569 (reference EP/DU.SN1/2)

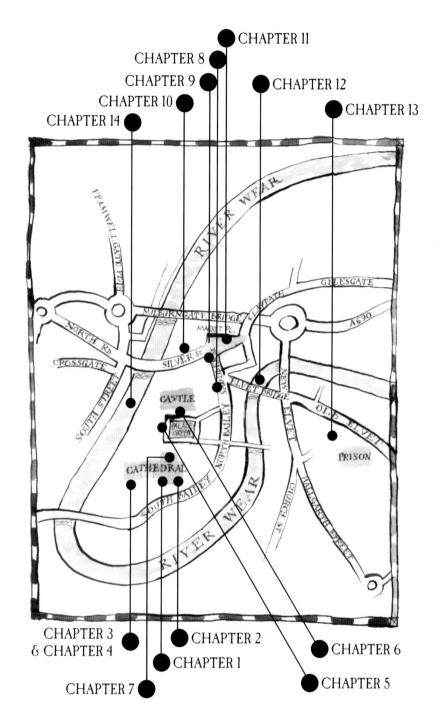

CHAPTER 11

CHAPTER 8

CHAPTER 9

CHAPTER 12

CHAPTER 10

CHAPTER 13

CHAPTER 14

CHAPTER 3
& CHAPTER 4

CHAPTER 2

CHAPTER 6

CHAPTER 1

CHAPTER 7

CHAPTER 5